NATIONAL GEOGRAPHIC

It's Dinner Time

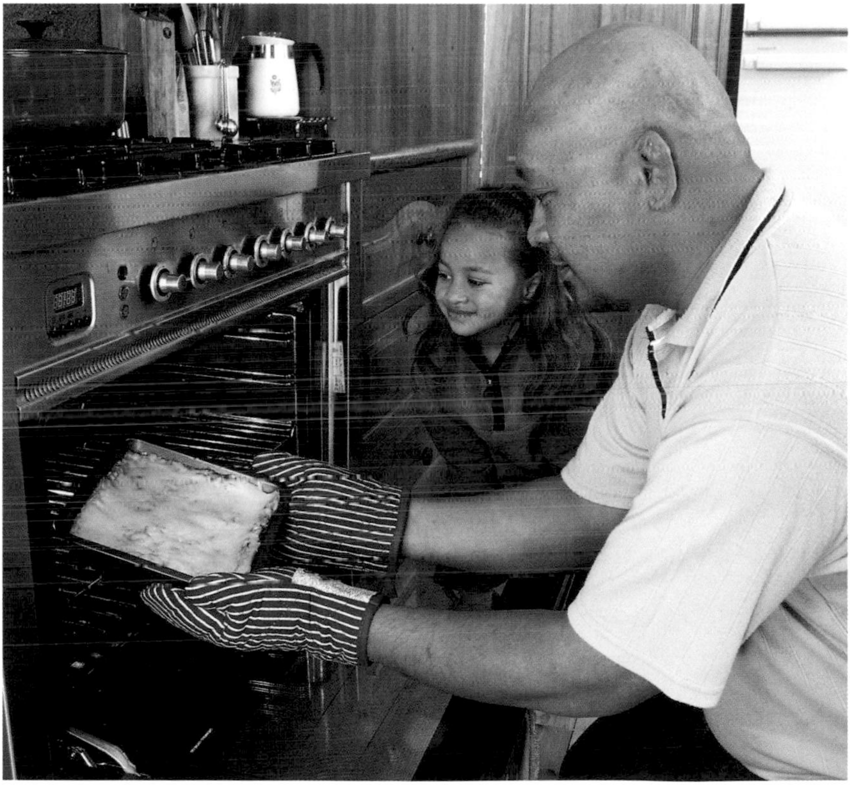

Ming Tan

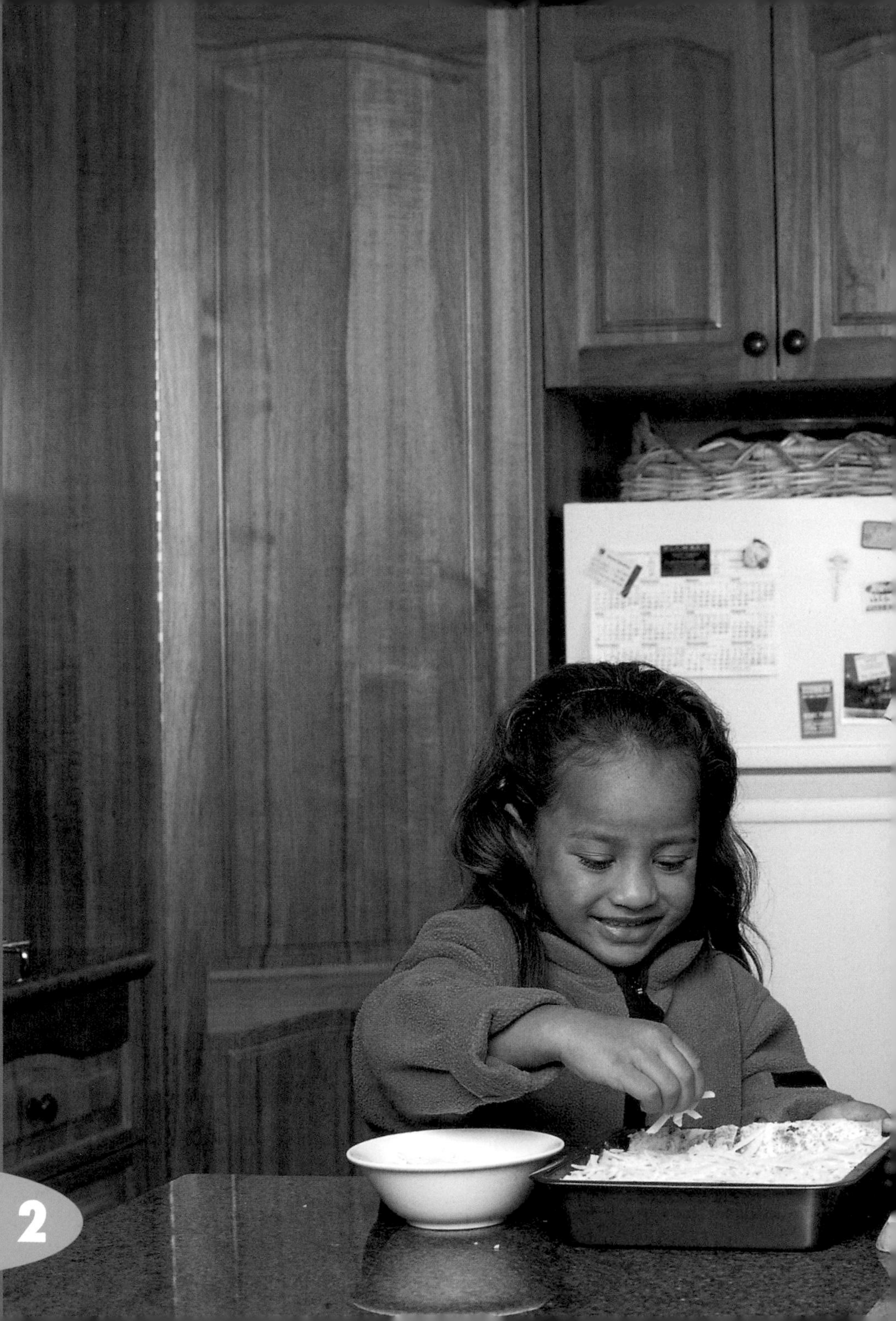

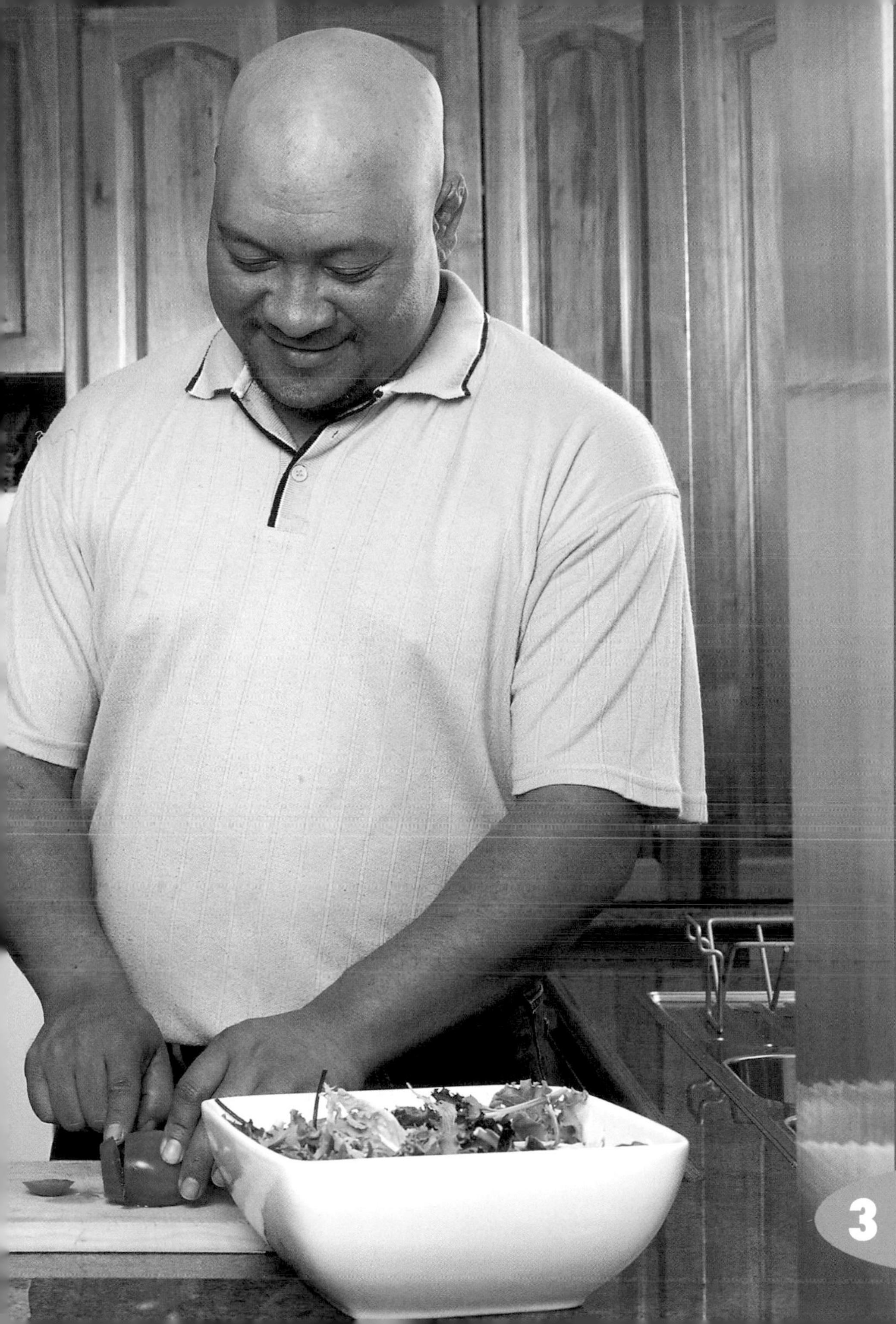

3

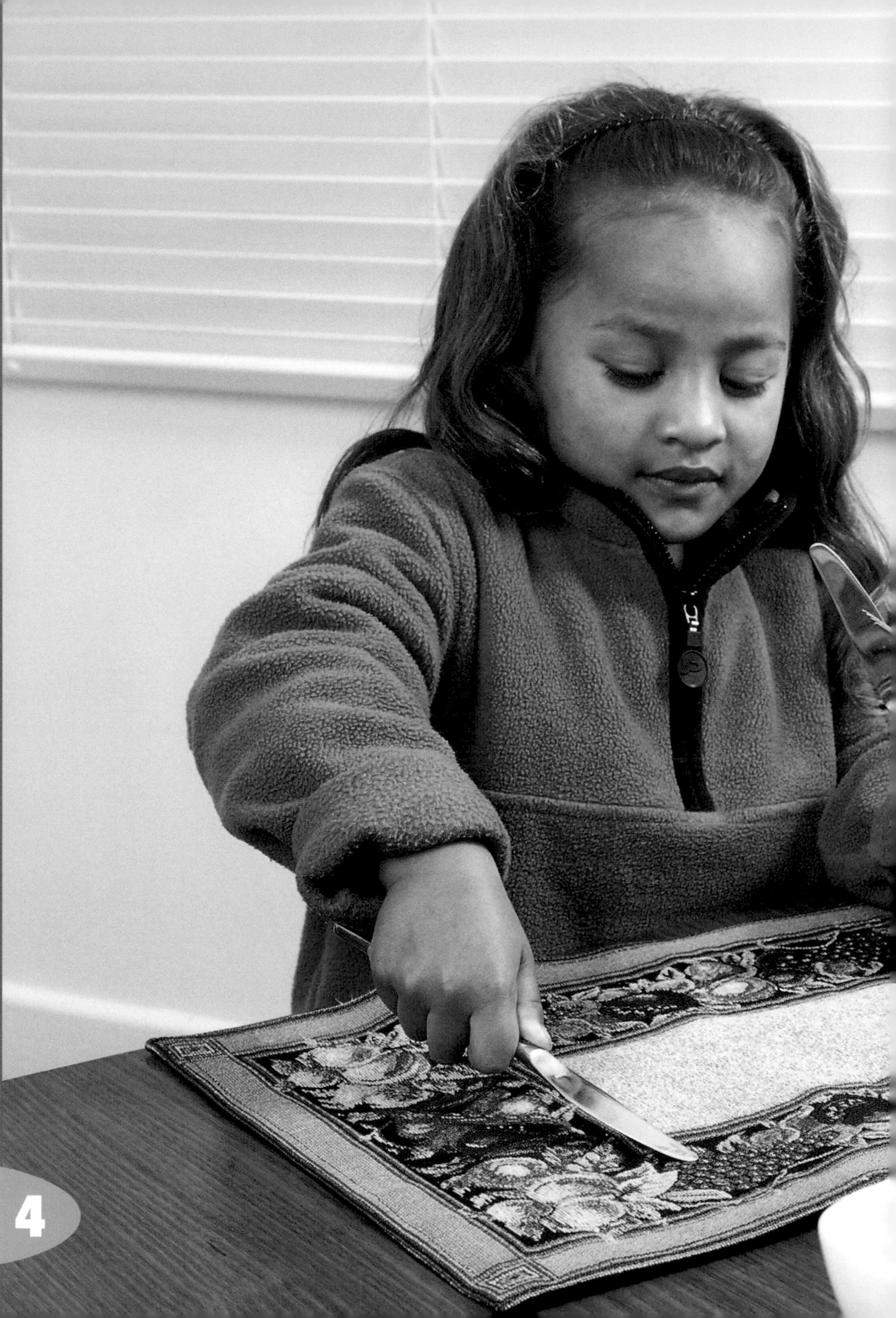

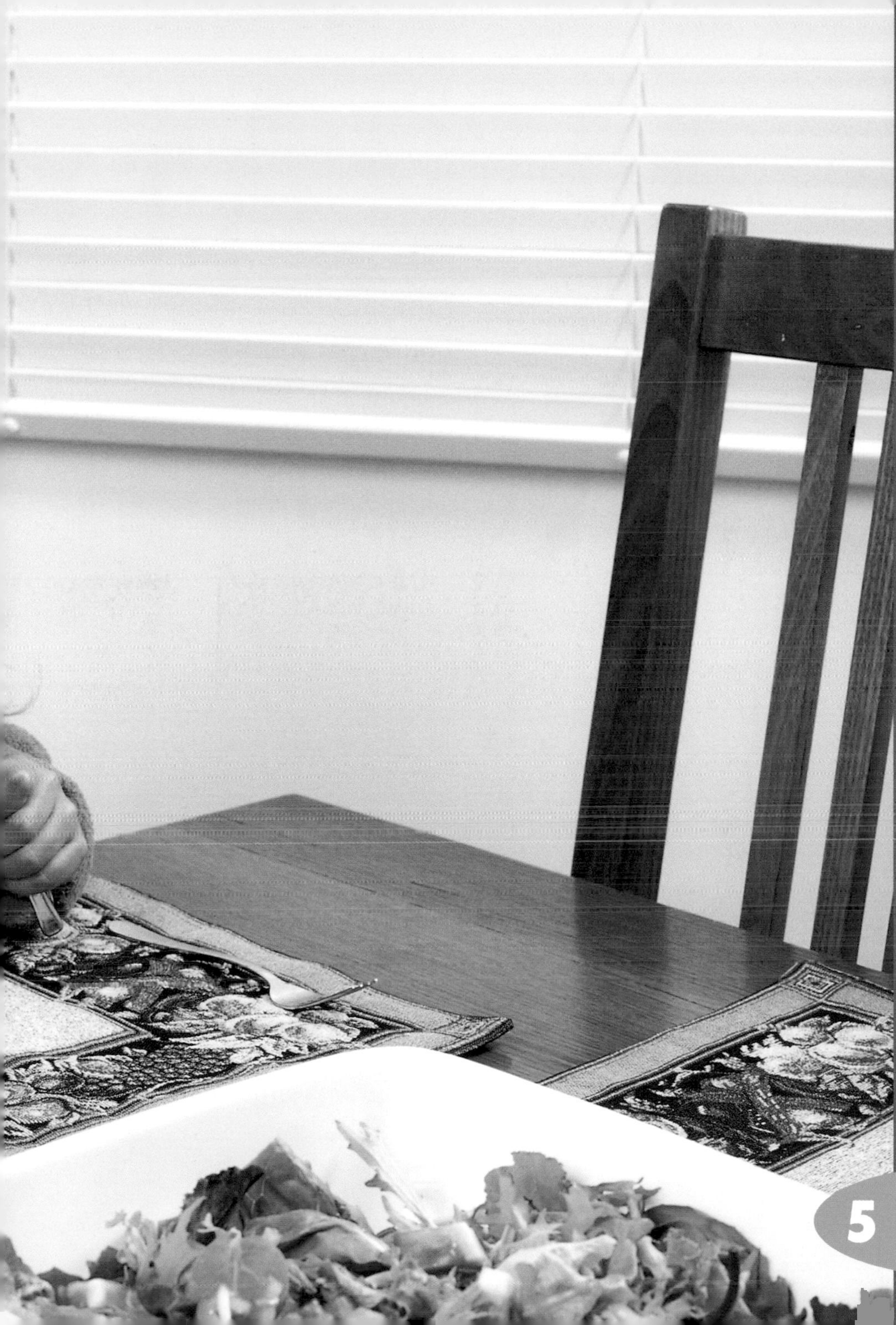

5

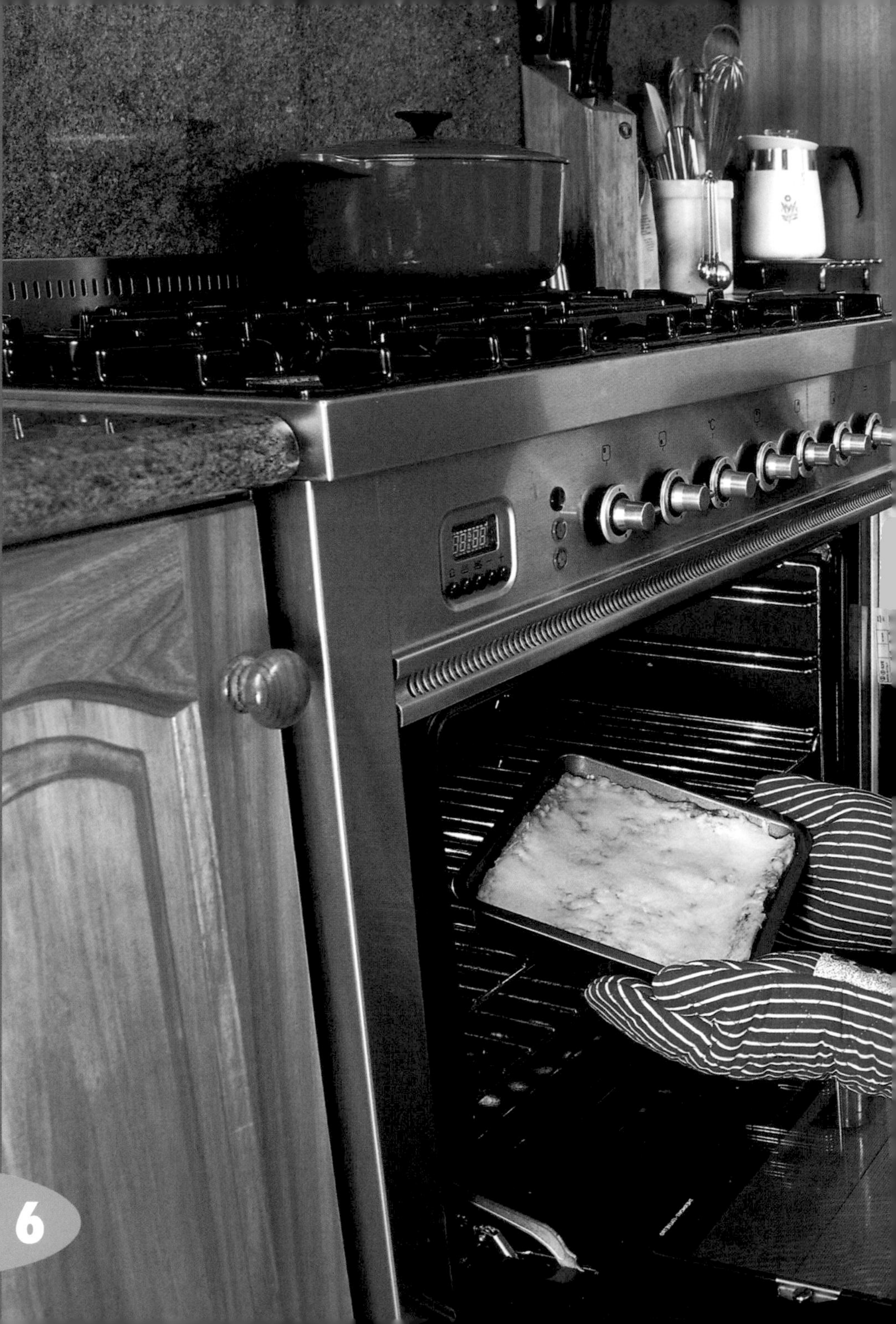

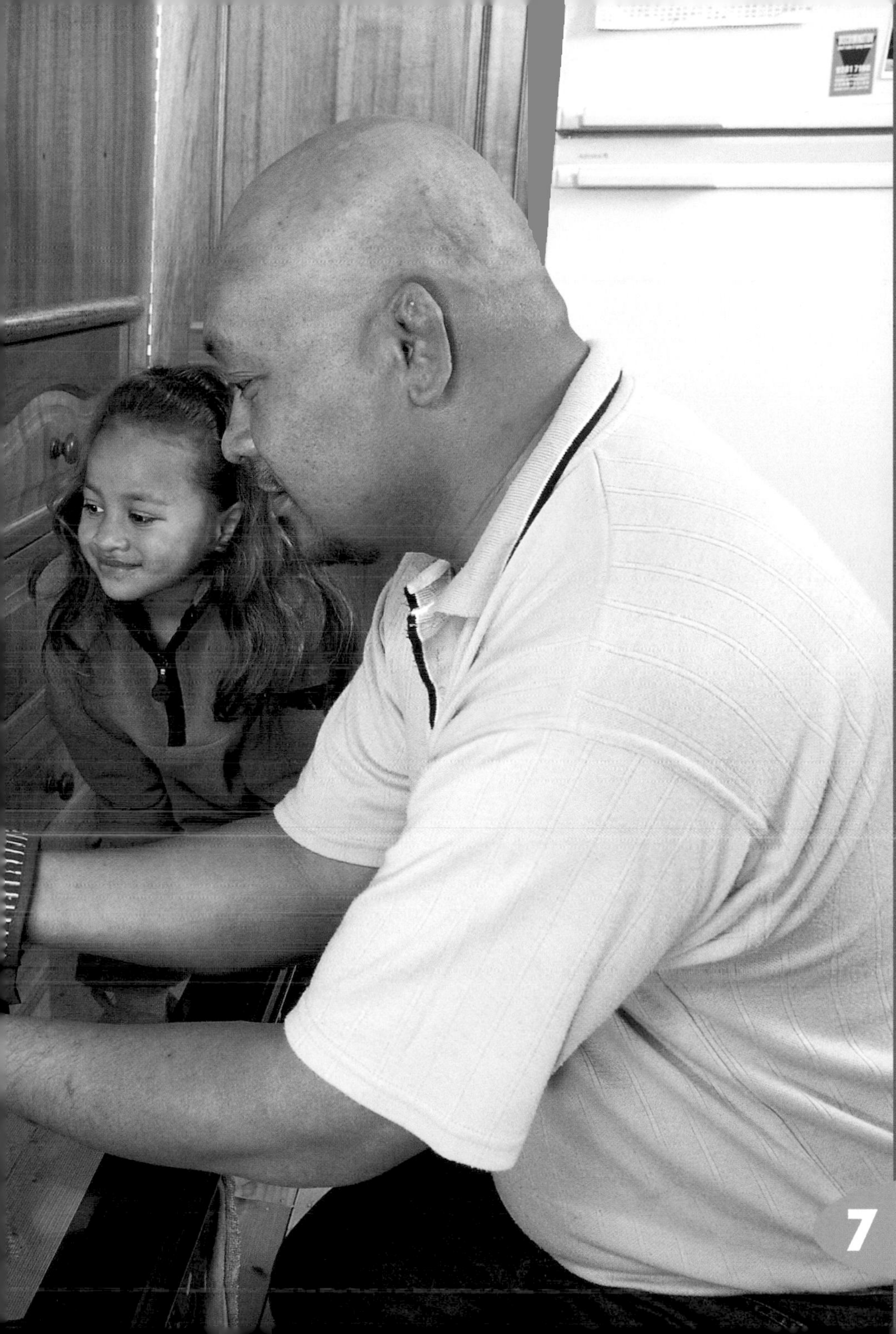

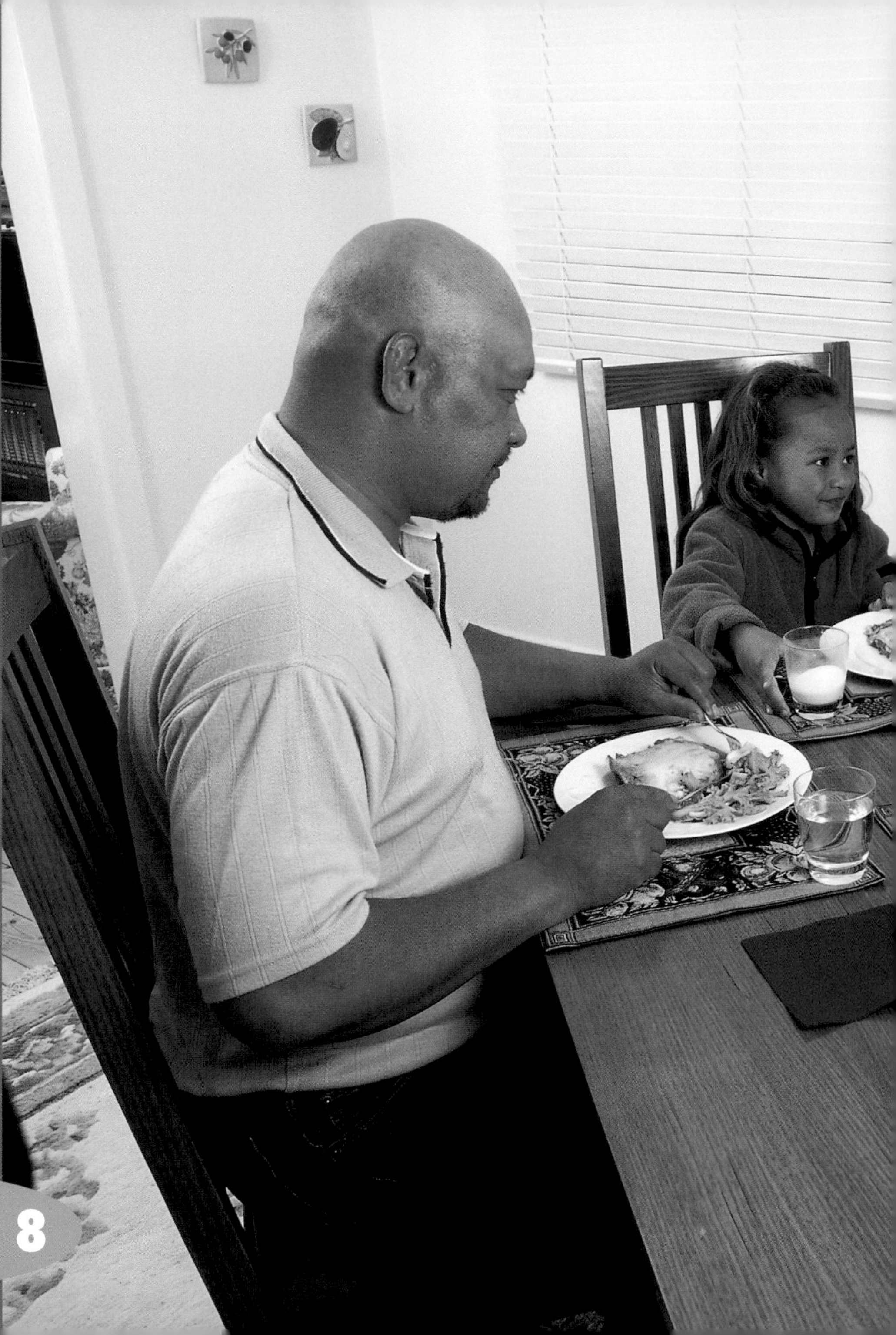

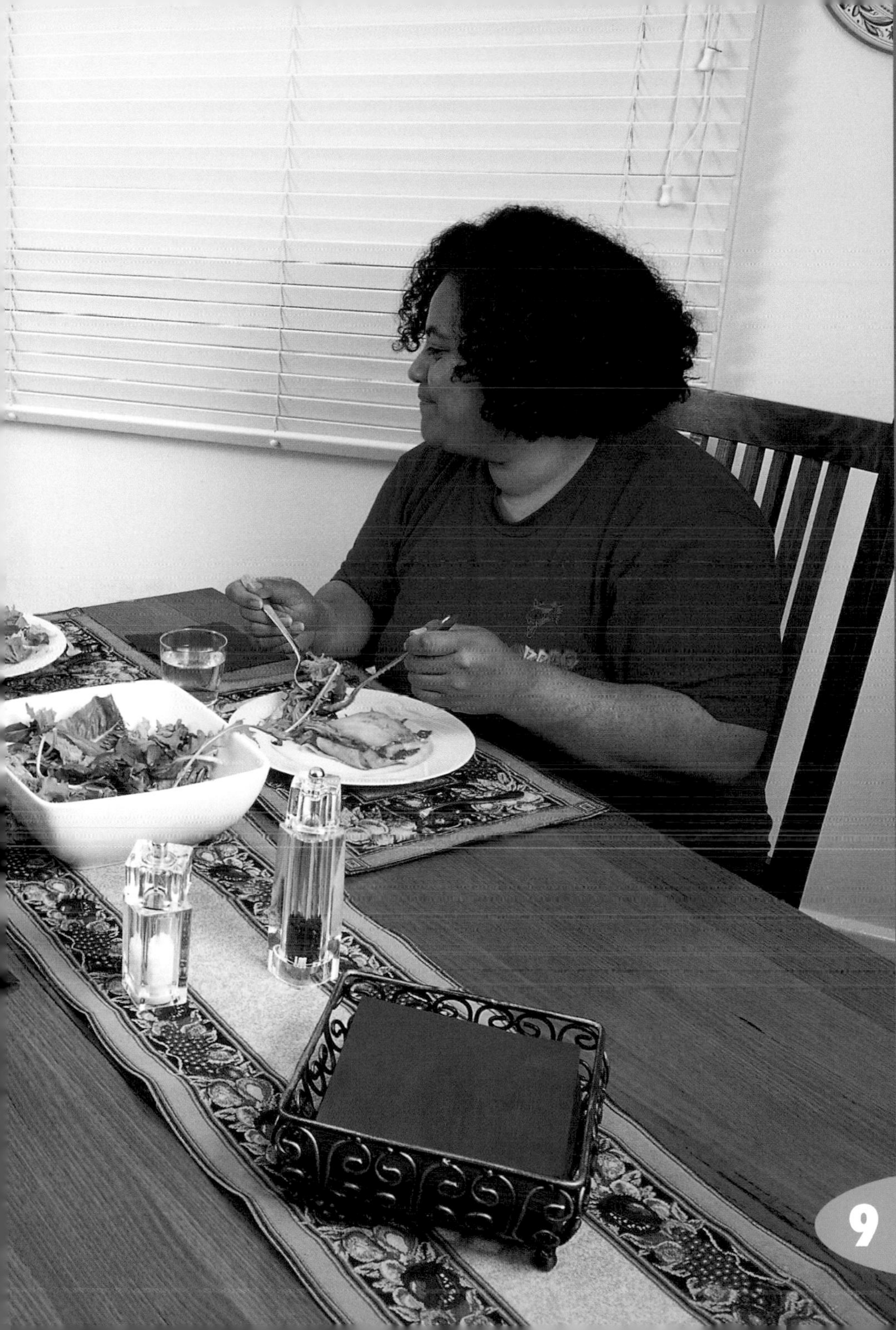

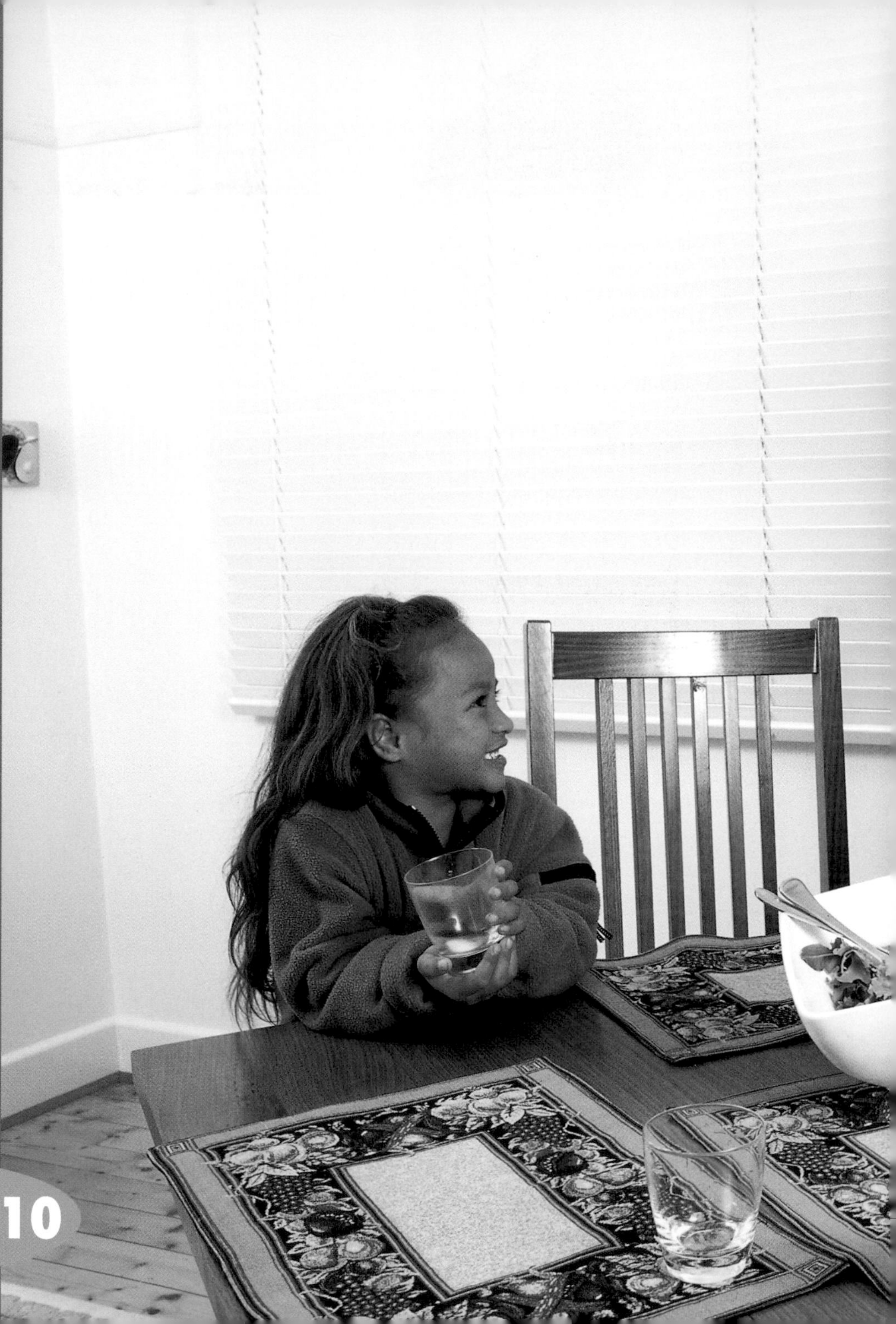

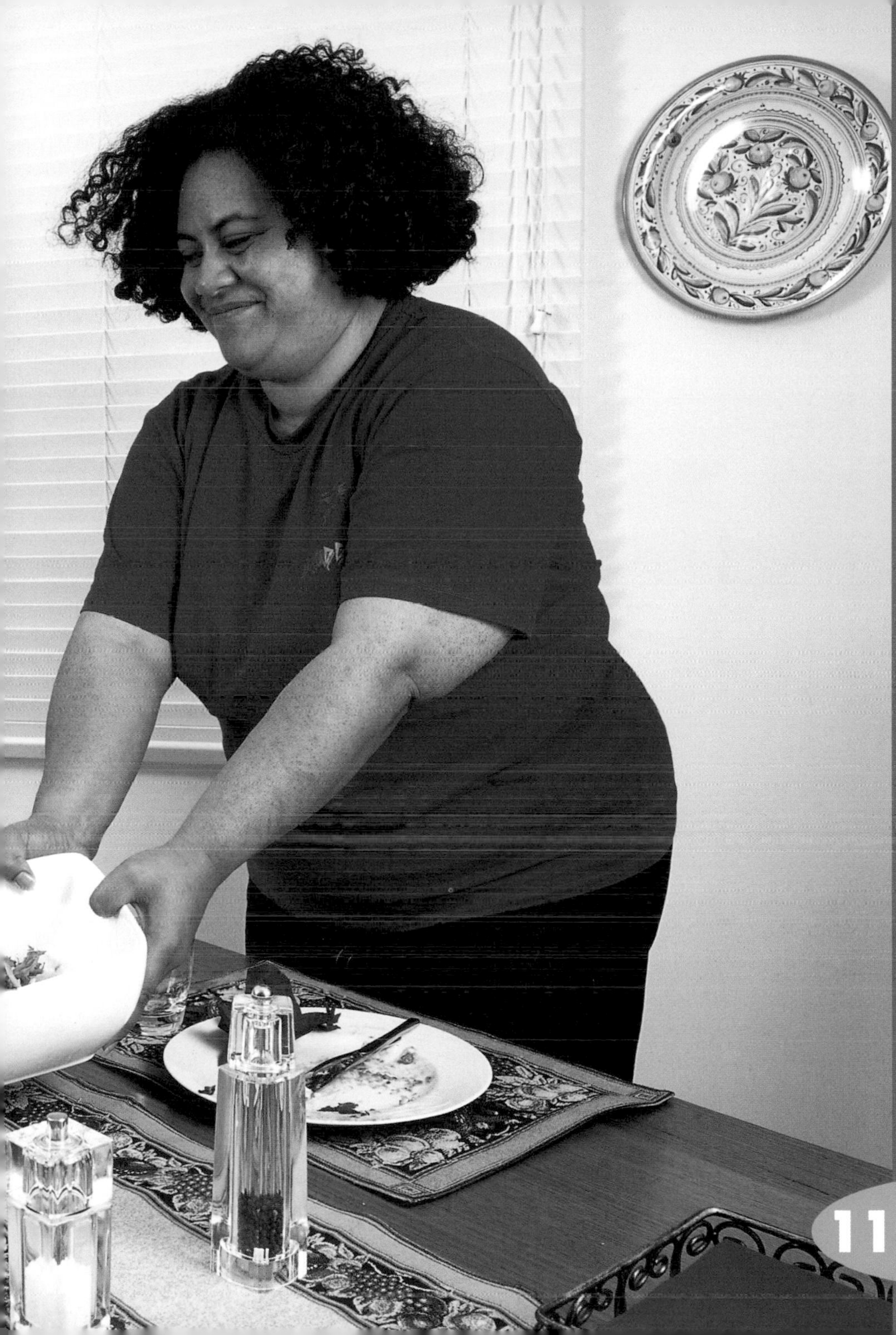

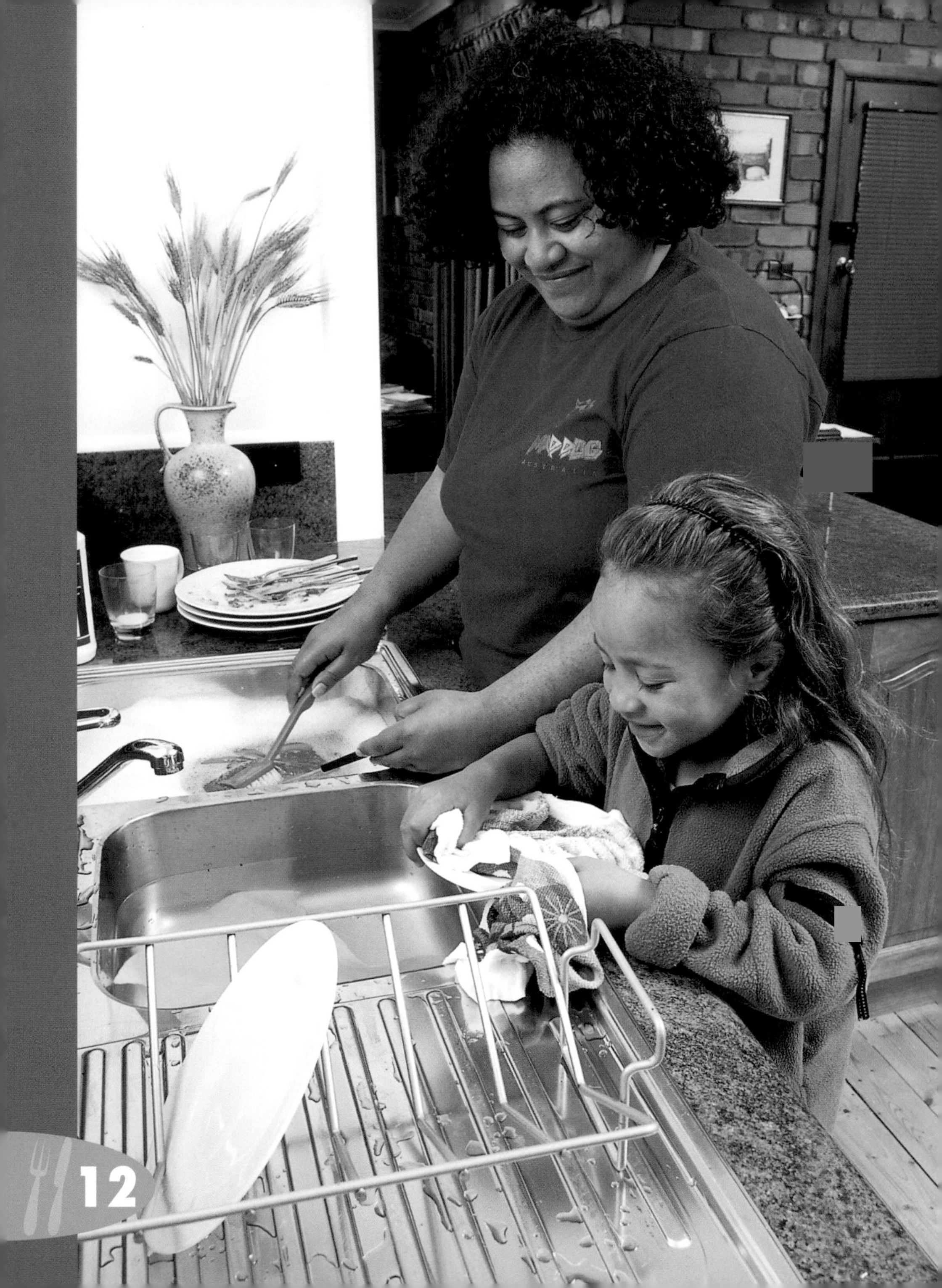